SRA
OPEN COURT
READING

Why, Bly?

A Division of The McGraw-Hill Companies

Columbus, Ohio

www.sra4kids.com

SRA/McGraw-Hill

A Division of The **McGraw·Hill** *Companies*

Send all inquiries to:
SRA/McGraw-Hill
8787 Orion Place
Columbus, OH 43240-4027

ISBN 0-07-569761-0
  2 3 4 5 6 7 8 9 DBH 05 04 03 02

Bly is an ostrich. She has a small head.
She likes to stick her head in dry sand.
Most animals feel that Bly is an odd bird.

"Bly, why do you stick your head
in dry sand?" asks Snake.
"Why not rest in the hot sun like me?"

"I do not like to rest in the hot sun," Bly says.
"I like myself just the way I am."

4

"Bly, why do you stick your head
in dry sand?" asks Chimp.
"Why not climb a tree like me?"

"I do not want to climb trees," Bly says.
"I like myself just the way I am."

"Bly, why do you stick your head
in dry sand?" asks Eagle.
"Why not fly in the sky like me?"

"I can't fly. I am too big," says Bly.
"I like myself just the way I am."

"Bly, why do you stick your head
in dry sand?" asks a child.
"Are you shy?"

"I am not shy," Bly says.

"It is hot and dry out here," Bly says.
"I feel better with my head stuck in the sand.
I will stay just the way I am."